W9-AIA-159

14.50

Everyday Science Experiments with Food

John Daniel Hartzog

The Rosen Publishing Group's
PowerKids Press™
New York

Some of the experiments in this book are designed for a child to do together with an adult.

Published in 2000 by The Rosen Publishing Group, Inc.
29 East 21st Street, New York, NY 10010

Photo Credits: Shalhevet Moshe

First Edition

Book Design: Michael de Guzman

Hartzog, John Daniel
      Everyday science experiments with food / by John Daniel Hartzog.
          p.   cm. — (Science surprises)
      Summary: Provides experiments that explore scientific phenomena occuring with food.
      ISBN 0-8239-5460-9 (alk. paper)
      1. Food—Experiments—Juvenile literature. 2. Science—Experiments—Juvenile literature. [1. Food—Experiments. 2. Science—Experiments. 3.
Experiments.] I. Title. II. Series: Hartzog, John Daniel. Science surprises.
TX355.H295   1999
507.8—dc21   99-13878
                                                        CIP

Manufactured in the United States of America

Contents

14.50

Experimenting with Food

Experimenting with food is one of the oldest forms of science around. People had to **experiment** to find out where to get the best foods, how to grow them, and how to cook them. Do you think when people first tried to make bread it came out just right? No, they had to try many times. They had to find out what worked and what didn't. People have always experimented with their food.

Any time you create an experiment you are working with science. Science isn't just something you learn in school. Science can be done with the foods you eat every day. These experiments will help you learn about food, but they will also help you learn about how other things in our world work.

◀ *People had to experiment to learn how to bake bread.*

Calcium Makes Strong Bones

When you eat chicken, you can see that the meat is attached to bones. These bones are like the ones we have in our bodies. Bones help us to stand up straight and give us our shape. **Calcium** is important for strong bones. All bones need calcium: human bones, dog bones, and chicken bones. Calcium is a **mineral** we get from foods like milk and green vegetables. Let's see what happens to a bone when you take away the calcium.

Next time your family is eating chicken, ask an adult

Materials Needed:
- A chicken bone
- A small glass or bowl
- Vinegar

This is what a chicken bone looks like naturally.

to remove all of the meat from one of the bones. Place the clean bone in a glass or bowl and cover it with vinegar. Set it aside somewhere where it will not be disturbed. Check the bone once a day for a week. Can you see it shrinking? The vinegar is an **acid**. The acid removes the calcium from the bone. The bone feels like rubber without the calcium to keep it strong. Imagine what your body would feel like if your bones had no calcium.

The bone looks much thinner and weaker without calcium. ▶

Materials Needed:
- 2 tablespoons of salt
- Dark-colored paper
- Scissors
- A saucer
- Half a cup of water

Be careful not to pour out any salt that might be at the bottom of the cup.

After the water evaporates, the salt is left on the paper in dry, crusty rings.

Pass the Salt

Salt helps give food flavor. People have used salt in their food for thousands of years. Salt can be found in the oceans and seas or where oceans and seas have dried up. Here is an experiment that shows how salt is formed.

Dissolve the salt in the water. You can't see the salt because it has dissolved in the water, but it's still there. Cut a piece of dark paper into a circle that fits into a saucer. Place the paper in the saucer and pour the **solution** over the paper. Leave the saucer in a safe spot for a few days. As the water **evaporates**, it leaves the salt in white, crusty rings on the paper. The salt we use in our food is formed in the same way when saltwater in the oceans and seas evaporates.

Making Butter

The butter that we eat comes from a cow's milk. When families had their own cow at home, they made their own butter. Butter is a fat that is **suspended** in cream. Butter

Materials Needed:
- Heavy cream
- A container with a tight-fitting lid

never really dissolves in the cream and when the cream warms just a little, the fat sticks together. Let's see if you can make this happen.

Fill a container a little more than halfway full with heavy cream. Screw the lid on as tight as you can. Now start shaking. You will need to shake the cream for around twenty

◄ *Pour the heavy cream into the container and screw the lid on tightly.*

minutes. A parent or a friend can take a turn if you get tired. As you shake, the cream will start to warm up. You can feel the butter begin to stick together. The lump of butter will get bigger and bigger. When the lump of butter stops growing, you will be left with butter and buttermilk. Pour out the contents of the container to separate the buttermilk from the butter. Now you can spread your butter on a slice of toast. Enjoy!

Shake well! ▶

Plastic Bag Farms

Have you ever seen old bread or cheese that has small spots of white or green hairy stuff on it? Gross, huh? Well, that stuff is alive and it is very natural. It is called mold. Mold is a fungus, a very small kind of plant, that helps things to **decompose**. All molds are not the same. Some are interesting and pretty. Some are gross. Let's see what kinds we can grow.

Pick three different kinds of food. You might try a small piece of bread, a slice of tomato, and a spoonful of cooked rice. Place each food in a different plastic bag. Leave the bags open for a day. This gives the fungus time

Materials Needed:
- 3 plastic bags
- Samples of 3 different foods
- A magnifying glass

to get inside the bags. Then seal the bags and watch your gardens grow. You will see spots of different colors and shapes appear on the food. Use a magnifying glass to investigate your mold farms through the plastic bags. The molds should all be different, with different colors and shapes. Can you describe the different molds? When you are finished with the experiment, throw the bags in the garbage.

Use a magnifying glass to examine the mold. ▶

Preserving Fruit

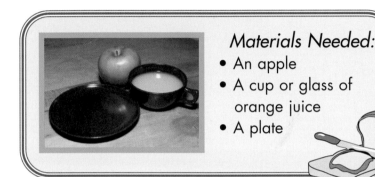

Materials Needed:
- An apple
- A cup or glass of orange juice
- A plate

Have you ever had apple slices in your lunch that have turned brown? Apples change when they touch the **oxygen** in the air. This is called oxidation. Most people do not like their food to change color, so scientists have discovered many ways to keep food fresh. People can add chemicals to **preserve** food. You probably have one natural food preservative at home: vitamin C. Let's see how vitamin C can preserve the white color of an apple.

Have an adult help you cut two slices from the same apple. Place one slice on a plate. Since orange juice is a good

◀ *Try to cover the whole slice with orange juice.*

source of vitamin C, dip the other slice in a cup or glass of orange juice before you put it on the plate. Check on the slices ten minutes after slicing. One apple slice should have turned brown, while the one you dipped in orange juice should still look white. The vitamin C preserves the apple by stopping the oxygen from turning it brown.

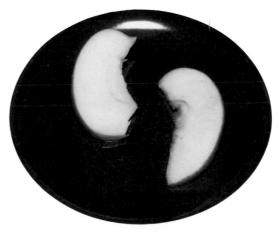

The slice that was dipped in orange juice will stay white while the other slice will turn brown. ▶

Materials Needed:
- A stove pot
- 1 cup of water
- 1 ½ cups of sugar
- String
- A pencil
- Paper clips
- A glass jar

Have an adult help you heat the water and dissolve the sugar.

▼

▲

The paper clips will weigh the strings so they hang straight down.

Making Crystals

Have you ever looked at salt or sugar close up? Salt and sugar are both **crystals**. Here is an experiment that will help you see what crystals look like. Ask an adult to heat the water on the stove. Add the sugar and stir until it has dissolved. Let the water cool for ten minutes. Pour the solution into a glass jar. Tie a few pieces of string to the middle of a pencil. Attach a paper clip to the end of each string. Place the pencil across the top of a jar and let the strings sink into the water. The paper clips will weigh the strings down so they hang straight. Leave the jar somewhere cool. Crystals will form on the strings as the water cools. These crystals are the same shape as normal sugar crystals, just bigger!

Homemade Soda

Materials Needed:
- A juice pitcher
- 2 tablespoons of powdered sugar
- 6 teaspoons of lemon juice
- 3 tablespoons of baking soda
- Food coloring (optional)
- Water

Have you ever wondered where soda bubbles come from? They come from **chemical reactions**. A chemical reaction is when something changes because of chemistry. In this experiment, lemon juice and baking soda will react to form soda.

Fill a pitcher full of water. Add the powdered sugar to the water. Add a few drops of food coloring if you choose to. Stir in the baking soda. Finally, add the lemon juice and stir. The mixture should start to bubble. Serve the soda quickly in glasses. The lemon juice is an acid. The baking soda is a **base**. Acids and bases are hydrogen-based solutions. The acid and the base chemically react to create a gas called carbon dioxide. Gas in a liquid makes bubbles.

Serve the soda quickly before it goes flat. ▶

◀ *Place the toothpicks around the center of the potato.*

Grow a Potato

Did you know that potatoes are full of energy that your body can use? The energy in a potato is used to help the potato plant to grow. Let's see the potato at work.

Take a potato and stick the four toothpicks around the center of it. Rest the toothpicks on the top of a jar or glass so that they are holding half of the potato in the water. Put the potato and the jar in a dark place (for the potato, the darkness will be like being underground where potatoes grow naturally). The potato will begin to sprout, or grow leaves. When the leaves are fully grown, put it in a window so it can get some sunlight. Now your potato is a plant!

You Are What You Eat

If you have done most of the experiments in this book, you have learned a lot about the foods you eat and where they come from. You made your own soda, your own butter, and even huge sugar crystals. You saw what happens to bones if they do not have enough calcium. You also grew molds in plastic bags. Even after seeing all these neat experiments, the most important thing you have done is learn about the everyday things around you through science. Science is a powerful tool that you can take anywhere and use anytime. Remember, keep observing and experimenting and you too will be a scientist. Good luck!

Glossary

acid (A-sid) A hydrogen-based solution that reacts with bases to form salt.

base (BAYS) A hydrogen-based solution that reacts with acids to form salt.

calcium (KAL-see-um) A chemical element that is found in teeth, bones, and certain kinds of rock.

chemical reactions (KEH-mih-kul ree-AK-shunz) A change in the chemical nature of two substances.

crystals (KRIS-tulz) The forms by which a variety of elements, including sugar and salt, turn to a solid state.

decompose (dee-cum-POHZ) To break down into more simple materials or rot.

dissolve (dih-ZOLV) To seem to disappear when mixed with a liquid.

evaporates (ee-VA-por-ayts) When water transforms from a liquid to a gas.

experiment (ehk-SPER-uh-ment) To test something out, or a test of something.

mineral (MIN-er-ul) A substance found in nature that is neither an animal nor a plant.

oxygen (AHKS-ih-jen) An invisible and odorless gas that animals need to stay alive.

preserve (pre-ZERV) To prepare food in order to save it for later use.

solution (suh-LOO-shun) A mixture of two substances, one of which dissolves in the other.

suspended (sus-PEN-dehd) When one substance floats in another.

Index

Web Sites:

You can learn more about food science on the Internet. Check out this Web site:
http://freeweb.pdq.net/headstrong